Whose Legs Are These?

A Look at Animal Legs—Kicking, Running, and Hopping

Written by Peg Hall
Illustrated by Ken Landmark

Whose Is It? Science

Content Advisor: Julie Dunlap, Ph.D.
Reading Advisor: Lauren A. Liang, M.A.
Literacy Education, University of Minnesota
Minneapolis, Minnesota

PiCTURE WiNDOW BOOKS
Minneapolis, Minnesota

Editor: Lisa Morris Kee

Designer: Melissa Voda

Page production: The Design Lab

The illustrations in this book were prepared digitally.

Printed in the United States of America.

Library of Congress Cataloging-in-Publication Data
Hall, Peg.
  Whose legs are these? : a look at animal legs—kicking, running, and hopping / written by Peg Hall; illustrated by Ken Landmark.
    p. cm. — (Whose is it?)
  Summary: Examines a variety of animal legs, noting how they look different and function in different ways.
  ISBN 1-4048-0007-7 (lib. bdg. : alk. paper)
  1. Leg—Juvenile literature. [1. Leg. 2. Animals.] I. Landmark, Ken, ill. II. Title.
QL950.7 .H35 2003
591.47'9—dc21   2002005777

Picture Window Books
5115 Excelsior Boulevard
Suite 232
Minneapolis, MN 55416
1-877-845-8392
www.picturewindowbooks.com

Step right up and see who's who.

Look closely at an animal's legs. Animals can have two legs, four legs, six legs, or more. Their legs can be longer than your whole body or shorter than your little finger.

Legs can tell how an animal finds food or stays safe from its enemies. Legs help animals walk, hop, leap, and swim. There are even legs that help an animal hear.

Legs don't all look alike, because they don't all work alike.

Can you tell whose legs are whose?

Look in the back for more fun facts about legs.

3

Whose legs are these, kicking in the water?

4

These are a frog's legs.

A frog has very strong back legs for jumping high and swimming fast. The frog's legs help it dart away from its enemies.

Fun fact: A baby frog does not have legs. It looks like a fish. A baby frog grows legs as it turns into an adult.

Whose legs are these, jumping through the grass?

7

These are a short-horned grasshopper's legs.

The male grasshopper chirps by rubbing his back legs against his front wings. That's how he talks to other grasshoppers.

Fun fact: Some grasshoppers use their legs to hear. A long-horned grasshopper's front legs have special parts that work like ears.

Whose legs are these, gliding through the air?

These are a flying squirrel's legs.

A flying squirrel has flaps of skin between its front and back legs. When the squirrel leaps from a tree, it spreads its legs wide. The extra skin stretches out like a parachute, and the squirrel glides through the air.

Fun fact: A flying squirrel can glide half the length of a football field. The squirrel steers by moving its legs and tail.

Whose legs are these, ready to pounce?

These are a cougar's legs.

The powerful hind legs of the cougar make it a dangerous hunter. The cougar can jump 30 feet (9 meters) in one great leap. It springs through the air, landing right on its next meal. The cougar's deadly pounce can crush small animals.

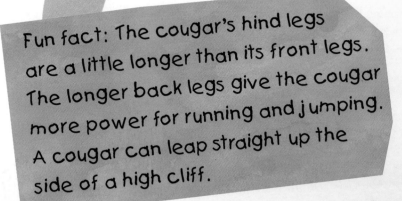

Fun fact: The cougar's hind legs are a little longer than its front legs. The longer back legs give the cougar more power for running and jumping. A cougar can leap straight up the side of a high cliff.

12

Whose legs are these, wading in the water?

These are a flamingo's legs.

A flamingo's legs are very long so it can wade in deep water to find food. A flamingo often stands on one leg, tucking the other foot under its body. That keeps the foot warm.

Fun fact: It looks like a flamingo has knees that bend backward, but the joints on a flamingo's long legs are not the bird's knees. They are its ankles.

Whose legs are these, covered with pollen?

These are a honeybee's legs.

A honeybee's legs are hairy. As the
honeybee buzzes from flower to flower,
dusty pollen sticks to the hairs. The pollen
rubs off on other flowers,
helping the flowers
make seeds.

Fun fact: The honeybee has
six legs. The two front legs
have special parts that work
like combs. The bee uses
these legs to clean its eyes
and its antennae.

Whose legs are these, standing so tall?

These are a giraffe's legs.

A giraffe's legs are taller than most people. The long legs and long neck of the giraffe help it reach tasty leaves on tall trees. A giraffe has to spread its legs far apart to bend down for a drink.

Fun fact: When attacked, the giraffe kicks with its strong legs. One kick can knock out a lion.

Whose legs are these, running down the street?

These are your legs!

Like other animals, you use your legs for walking, running, and jumping. Your legs can bend at the knees and turn at the hips. Your legs push you through the water when you swim. You can crouch, crawl, skip, and strut. What else do you do with your legs?

If your legs had flaps, would you glide through the air? If your legs were tall, would you wade in the water? Would you rather leap like a cougar or swim like a frog?

Just for Fun

The number of an animal's legs can tell you a lot about the animal family it belongs to. For example, all insects have six legs. All birds have two legs. Lots of other animals have four. Using your finger, trace a line between the animal and its correct number of legs.

flamingo   giraffe   honeybee

4   6   2

Fun Facts About Legs

LONG LEGS Lying down to take a nap isn't easy for a giraffe. The giraffe leans down on its front legs, then it stretches out one long hind leg. It tucks the other hind leg under its body. It's hard for the giraffe to get up again, too. A giraffe usually lies down only when other giraffes stand guard, watching for danger.

HAIRY LEGS The Chilean rose tarantula is a large, hairy spider. The tarantula uses the hair on its legs to help it find prey. The leg hair can sense the movement of small insects in the air.

LEGS THAT HIDE Some animals can hide their legs when they feel threatened. A painted turtle can pull its head and legs inside its shell if danger is near. A ladybug can pull its six legs completely inside its body and pretend to be dead.

FAST LEGS The cheetah is the fastest runner on Earth. It can race as fast as a car on the highway. For about half the time a cheetah is running, all four legs are in the air at the same time. A cheetah seems to fly.

CRAZY LEGS Each of a spider's eight legs can bend in six places. That means a spider has 48 separate knees. Spiders use their bendable legs to walk, jump, and build complicated webs. When an insect is caught in a web, the web moves a little. The spider can feel the movement through its legs. If a spider loses a leg in a fight, the spider will grow a new leg.

LEGS THAT JUMP A leopard frog can jump a distance 12 times the length of its body. That's like you being able to jump across a four-lane highway. A few frogs can leap 20 times their body length.

Words to Know

antennae Antennae are feelers on an insect's head.

hind legs Hind legs are back legs.

joint A joint is a bendable place in a body. Knees, hips, and ankles are joints.

pollen Pollen is a fine powder found in the middle of flowers.

prey Prey are animals that are hunted and eaten by other animals.

23

To Learn More

AT THE LIBRARY

Davis, Katie. **Who Hops?** San Diego: Harcourt
Brace, 1998.

Fowler, Allan. **Arms and Legs and Other
Limbs.** New York: Children's Press, 1999.

Hickman, Pamela. **Animals in Motion: How
Animals Swim, Jump, Slither, and Glide.**
Toronto: Kids Can Press, 2000.

Royston, Angela. **Life Cycle of a Frog.**
Des Plaines, Ill.: Heinemann Library, 1998.

ON THE WEB

Lincoln Park Zoo
http://www.lpzoo.com
Explore the animals at the Lincoln Park Zoo.

San Diego Zoo
http://www.sandiegozoo.org
Learn about animals and their habitats.

Want to learn more about animal legs?
Visit FACT HOUND at
http://www.facthound.com

Index

ankle, 14

antennae, 16

birds, 21

cheetah, 22

Chilean rose
  tarantula, 22

cougar, 11–12, 20

flamingo, 13–14, 21

flying squirrel, 9–10

frog, 4–6, 20, 23

giraffe, 17–18, 21, 22

grasshopper, 7–8

hips, 20

honeybee, 15–16, 21

insect, 21

joint, 14

knee, 14, 20, 23

ladybug, 22

pollen, 15, 16

spider, 22, 23

turtle, 22